Dedication

Dedicated to my parents, Anne and Norman Baines, who loved and supported each other throughout their lifetimes and bequeathed the values they cherished: knowing who you are; the importance of family; believing that anything is within your grasp; the importance of education and hard work; humor; taking time to enjoy life; and "the beauty part of it".

The Ethical Will Resource Kit

Preserving Your Legacy of Values For Your Family

An Introduction To Ethical Wills With Step-by-Step Instructions and Exercises To Help You Prepare One

Barry K. Baines, MD

Published by Josaba Limited.

1629 West 25th St.

Minneapolis, MN 55405

Printed in the United States of America

ISBN 0-9676794-0-0

The Ethical Will Resource Kit

Contents

Page

Introduction

Most people are familiar with the concept of a "last will and testament". It is the means of distributing our accumulated assets to our loved ones and favorite charities, and to effect other important decisions at the time of our death.

But...have you ever considered writing an ethical will?

In a metaphorical way, an ethical will is a way to "bequeath your values" in the same way that a will of inheritance provides for bequeathing your valuables. Unlike wills of inheritance which divide things, an ethical will is a way to share; your values, beliefs, hopes for the future, life's lessons, stories, love, and forgiveness with your family and community. Writing an ethical will places our lives in the broader context of continuity; a linkage from past to future generations.

Although many cultures have the tradition of naming children in honor of deceased and living relatives, many of us have no written history to connect us to our namesakes.

Have you ever discovered a letter from a relative whom you never knew? It's incredible how the smallest bits and pieces of information about their lives rekindle and strengthen your feelings of connection to your ancestors. An ethical will can provide a storehouse of information for present and future generations.

Ethical wills are no new invention. Hebrew scripture first described the tradition of ethical wills or *tzava'ah*, which were transmitted verbally. The most common biblical references that are viewed as examples of ethical wills are Genesis, 49, Deuteronomy, 32 and 33, and John "x". Later, they were written as a codicil (or attachment) to wills of inheritance, or as a separate document. There are ethical wills preserved from as far back as the medieval and renaissance periods

The contents of ethical wills can be variable. In general they usually addressed personal values and life principles, hopes for future generations, asking forgiveness and forgiving others, and even burial instructions.

There are many reasons to write an ethical will. Here is a list of some of the more common ones:

- When you write an ethical will, you learn a lot about yourself
- It is a way to affirm the past and be positive about the future
- It allows for putting your personal "signature" on what universal values mean to you (e.g., love, truth)
- It opens the door to forgiving others and being forgiven, which heals relationships
- It helps coming to terms with our mortality
- It's easier to write a will of inheritance and a living will (advance directives) when you know what principles are important to you
- It can be a spiritual experience that provides a sense of completion in our lives
- If we don't preserve our stories no one else will, and future generations will be deprived of this precious history

Ethical wills were originally associated with someone's final days. However, with the revival of this tradition, they are being written to mark other family and life cycle events.

For those of us not thinking of death as being near at hand, by writing an ethical will we can step back and reflect on what we stand for and what we value most in our lives. It can provide us with the opportunity to plan our lives with living our values as a goal.

Many of us try our best to live our values on a day to day basis, but sometimes we don't succeed as often as we'd like to. By documenting the values that are important to us, we can focus on them, and, at the same time, clarify our belief system for our families.

Some clergy encourage soon-to-be-married couples to write an ethical will, and use it as a basis for how they will raise a family. The birth of a child also provides an opportunity for a couple to take pause and reflect on values important to them as they embark upon the challenging journey of parenting.

Even in divorce, an ethical will can provide some level of security for children who are often in a difficult situation, by giving them some measure of knowing the values their parents aspire to.

Some legal professionals have begun recommending to clients to write and add an ethical will to their legal wills. Estate planners are also using the ethical will to help people identify values important to them for the purpose of planned charitable giving.

Every ethical will is as unique as the person writing it. Having reviewed a number of written ethical wills before writing my own, I was struck by the fact that whether simple or elegant, all conveyed the sense of coming from the heart.

My work with hospice patients heightened my awareness of my own mortality. In my role as medical director of a home-based hospice program, I have seen a theme that is often repeated by people as they face the end of their lives: to provide a legacy of personal and spiritual values, hopes, experiences, love, and forgiveness, to their family and future generations.

People want to be remembered after they are gone.

This underscored the importance of leaving a record for my family of what's really important to me. Life is fragile, and none of us know how much time we really have in our lifetime. This introspection provided me with the impetus to write my own ethical will.

For my family, there were few, if any surprises when they read my ethical will. However, it did leave my children speechless to actually see my beliefs, values and hopes in written form. It was clear to me that this was viewed as a precious gift.

Trying to write an ethical will can seem difficult. I believe there are several barriers that prevent us from undertaking this task.

One reason is that our Western society reinforces the denial of death as a natural part of life. It takes much courage to sit down and admit that indeed, we are mortal.

Even if we manage to face our own mortality, there is another barrier many people encounter- self-doubt. Thinking, “I’m not a good enough writer to do this”, or “I might be embarrassed by doing this”, can be a real impediment.

The final barrier is our culture’s love affair with technology. The arrival of VCR’s, camcorders, audio cassettes and CD’s have practically placed the art of letter-writing on the endangered species list.

I hope this information will provide the spark you need to consider taking on the challenge of writing your ethical will. It may well be one of the most valuable gifts you can give to your family.

“And make these things known to your children and to your grandchildren.” (Maimonides, Hilchot Talmud Torah 1:2)

By Barry K. Baines, MD

How to Write an Ethical Will

Now that you have made the decision that you want to try to write your ethical will, there are a number of simple steps you can take to write it. As you will see, it isn't very difficult to do.

If you think you would have a hard time doing this yourself, ask a family member to help you. Surely a spouse, child, grandchild or friend would be honored to help you reach your goal.

Collecting ideas

To start with, it's helpful to write down some of your ideas on paper. This can be a sentence or two, or just a few words. Write down each idea on a separate piece of paper or use "Post-it™" notes.

I found it helpful to group my ideas in different categories, e.g., personal values, my hopes for the future, and personal experiences

Two other ways to group your ideas are:

- My beliefs and opinions
- My actions (things I did to act on my beliefs and opinions)
- What I've learned from life
- What I've learned from you
- What my dreams are for you
- What my blessings are for you

or

You can also group your thoughts and feelings in terms of:

- Personal ideas
- Family ideas
- Spiritual ideas

Here are some exercises that will help you to generate ideas for your ethical will.

On a sheet of paper, write examples for the following:

- Something I learned from my grandparents
- Something I learned from my parents
- Something I learned from my spouse/children/siblings
- Something I learned from experience
- Something I am grateful for

Write stories about important events in your life as you remember them:

- What values are illustrated by these stories?
- Here are 4 "universal" values: love, beauty, truth, and justice. Write a story from your life experiences that provide your unique perspective of any or all of these values.

Think about critical decisions you've made throughout your life.

- Why are you glad you made them?
- What would you have done differently in retrospect?
- What positive actions can you undertake now? (this is a good exercise for healing and repairing relationships)

If you only had a limited time left to live, what would be important for you to do with the time you have left? What will be said at your funeral? In answering these questions, you will see what things you truly value. This will quickly put you in touch with those values worthy of transmitting to your family.

Here's another method for collecting ideas:

Start "journaling"

- Write about events, thoughts, and feelings that strike you as important, and place these in a folder
- Save items that articulate your feelings, e.g. quotes, cartoons, etc.
- In a few months, take some time off and review what you've collected or written
- As you examine this information, you'll see items that are related
- Clump these similar words, phrases, etc., together
- Important values and patterns will naturally emerge from all that you've collected
- Connect these thoughts into sentences, and the sentences into paragraphs
- Arrange the paragraphs in an order that is comfortable
- Add an introduction and a conclusion.

Putting it all together

It might seem hard to know how to begin the actual writing of your ethical will.

To help you with this task, I have included several resources:

- A step-by-step exercise for writing your first draft
- A copy of several modern ethical wills
- References for further reading about ethical wills and related topics

I believe many people want to preserve their values, experiences and hopes for future generations. As our modern society places more emphasis on material things, it's easy to lose sight of what we think is really important in our lives.

Recording these thoughts and feelings in this way might be one of the most meaningful gifts you can give to your family. Let your ethical will speak from your heart. Best of luck.

Creating Your First Draft

Facing a blank piece of paper is probably the biggest barrier you will have to overcome in writing your ethical will. To help you get over this hurdle, I have put together some general topic areas that identify some specific values that may be important to you.

Completing this exercise will give you an initial draft of your ethical will from which to work. I know this was helpful for me in bridging the gap from blank page to finished product.

These "thought-starters" are in no particular order. When you go through the ethical will after you have a working draft, you can move things around so they are in an order that makes sense to you.

You might want to consider whether you plan on presenting your ethical will to your family during your lifetime or after your death. This draft is written with the intent of passing it on while still alive.

Possible openings for your ethical will

- To my family:
- To my dearest family:
- Dear . . . (use actual names of people you want to give your ethical will to):
- To the people who are most important to me :

As I think about my life, I want to tell you about some of . . .

- my experiences
- the things that I value
- the things I believe in
- the things that I did
- the lesson's I've learned from life
- the things that had the biggest impact on who I am as a person

Life experiences

Tell about some of your life experiences. These memories-particular events, mishaps, and successes, will help you see the patterns that shaped your life. For example, write some stories about where you grew up and experiences with your family that stand out in your mind.

Here's an example of a story about growing up:

I grew up in Brooklyn, NY. I lived on the upper floor of a duplex apartment with my parents and my younger brother. My aunt and uncle and their two kids lived downstairs. We took vacations together every summer in the Catskill Mountains in upstate New York.

My grandparents only lived a few blocks from our house, so I saw them several times a week. When my grandma was unable to live by herself in her apartment, she moved in with us.

Being close to family was always important to me. I hope you stay close to each other after I'm gone.

Stories about jobs you had or how you chose your occupation.

Here's an example of a story about jobs I had earlier in my life:

I worked from the time I was in high school. I sold newspapers, worked in a candy store (that's what they called soda fountains in Brooklyn), and did some office work all through college. From working with people, I knew I wanted to work where I could help people.

It's important to choose an occupation that you really enjoy-even if it takes a while to figure out what you want to do.

Values and Beliefs

"I've always valued" or "These are the values that I believe in":

- being honest
- keeping your word
- being dependable,
- helping others in need
- learning from your mistakes
- having a sense of humor

use other items from your list!

Here's one example of what I did to act on my beliefs.

I've always felt that helping others in need and volunteering to support your community are important personal values.

While training to be a physician, I volunteered some of my time working in a migrant workers clinic. The migrant workers didn't have any health insurance or easy access to medical care. They often went without needed health care in order to support their families. They were so grateful for any medical services, I really felt like I was making a difference in their lives.

I hope you will experience this same feeling of making a difference in other people's lives. There are many opportunities for this. You usually receive more than you give whenever and wherever you volunteer your time to help others in need.

Describe what you've learned from life

- Do you have some favorite sayings and examples of how they guided you?
- What are you most proud of? Your work? Your family? Your interests?
- What activities did you devote your time too and why?

These are all important to pass on to your loved ones.

Here's an example of a saying I'm fond of:

"Learning is a lifelong occupation".

I love to learn new things all the time. I've found that the more I learn, the better I understand myself and others.

Wishes for the future

"My hopes" or "My dreams", are for you:

- to continue the family tradition of....
- to establish a family
- to stay involved with......
- to be successful in ......
- to follow the observances of our religion

Write about things you haven't done yet or regret not having done. This can be a time of asking for understanding or forgiveness, forgiving others, providing guidance or "words of wisdom".

Summing up

- Thank you for your love and support through the years
- I love you all very much
- Think of me when you . . .

I believe that if you can walk yourself through this exercise, you will have a good starting point for your ethical will. These are very personal and meaningful documents, so be sure to write about what is important to you. The wording of your ethical will reflects the voice of your heart.

Examples of Modern Ethical Wills

This ethical will was written by a 47 year-old father of two teenage daughters.

To my family:

In reading my ethical will, I hope that you find very few surprises. I believe I've been open about the things that I've valued over time. I've also tried to live my values on a day-to-day basis. I trust that I succeeded much more often than I've failed.

As I matured and accumulated life experience (and life is a great teacher), I think I gained an appreciation of the importance of balance in my life. Balance among the family, work, spiritual, and physical aspects of life. And, having fun. It's easy to let things get out of balance. When they do, life can get out of control and become miserable. Always try to maintain a balance in your life.

Having a good sense of humor is very important. I know you've all moaned and groaned at my puns from time to time. Overall, the laughter was well worth it. It's important to have fun and there is humor in almost all aspects of life.

It's impossible to be successful in everything you try to do. So, don't be afraid of making mistakes. Just be sure you learn something from them. Sometimes you can learn more from a mistake than from always doing everything right.

Respect life- yours and others. I'm a believer in the idea of treating other people the way you want to be treated. This is the proverbial "Golden Rule".

My hopes (to you, Alisha and Hannah), are that you find a vocation that adds value to the world. This is my interpretation of Tikkun Olam. I feel very lucky to have worked in the hospice world and devoting some of my energies to issues people face at the end of life. I think trying to relieve suffering has been a worthwhile pursuit for me.

I hope you continue the traditions and faith of Judaism. Although this spiritual aspect of myself was relatively unimportant to me in my younger years, I feel you all have a wonderful foundation and excellent skills and knowledge in regard to the basic tenets of Judaism. I hope you will be able to pass these on to future generations.

I hope you are as lucky as I was in finding a soulmate like Sandy to share your life with; someone with whom to enjoy time together, grow together, solve problems together, face challenges together, support each other, and laugh and love together. It may not last forever, but the effort of staying together is worth it.

As I look back over my life, overall, I am happy with what I've accomplished. I've tried many things and would like to try some more. As long as you live you can always learn new things. This is an important value to cherish.

One of my regrets is that my parents and father-in-law weren't around to share in some of the things we (as a family) have done over the past 5-10 years. Another regret is not spending even more time together as a family. We certainly have taken some incredibly fun vacations: our three car trips (to the west coast, Canada and Niagara Falls, Hershey-Gettysburg-Washington DC-Williamsburg), Pinehurst, and of course Italy. I'm glad we kept journals for all of them. You kids just grow up so fast, and before you know it, you're out there, (or soon will be) and on your own.

You all have been a great source of joy and strength for me. I love you all very much.

Dad

This is an ethical will written by a widowed mother and grandmother. She is in her early sixties.

To My Children and Grandchildren:

<u>My Family</u>

I had a special relationship with my grandmother. She lived next door to us and taught modesty, moderation and strength by personal example. From her I learned that one should "do good for the sake of good, not for the sake of reward" and that "there is no end of good that can be done by those who don't care who gets the credit."

<u>Learning and Knowledge</u>

These two keep us mentally sharp, keep us open to growth and change, enable us to contribute professionally and personally, and can provide us with pleasant hours. I believe, as my mother did, that hard work and intelligence can go far to overcoming many problems.

It is a privilege to be able to share your knowledge and your love of learning with others. I have been fortunate to find many opportunities for teaching, both formal and informal.

<u>Taking and Giving</u>

In giving you make your life worthwhile. But if you don't take, you will have nothing to give. Don't refuse to accept: others need a chance to give also.

I hope you will make the world a better place, both on a smaller scale and in the wider sense. Try to be a part of the solution, not part of the problem. Keep before you for inspiration a vision of the way things ought to be and help us move, albeit so slightly, in that direction.

Appreciation and Love

My children, you are sources of joy and pride. You make me feel loved and cared for. Your thoughtfulness is touching and our interactions are a pleasure for me.

My love for my grandchildren is too great to express in words. I hope I have expressed it in other ways. Your existence gives me hope for the future and our mutual love gives me the greatest happiness."

The following ethical will was written by a 70 year-old father and grandfather to his son and daughter-in-law. He died of lung cancer about one month after this was written.

Dear Keith and Leigh:

A few words to express my feelings and thoughts while time is running out on me.

Some standard values that I have basically lived by throughout my life, are that I have always believed in honesty and advocated truthfulness. I cherish the family with all my heart. I always felt that I gave of myself to everyone in the family. The satisfaction and gratification that I received in return is in the accomplishments of my children. No father could be as proud as your father is of you. Throughout your lifetime so far, you have more than exceeded my greatest expectations. You continue to move forward in a manner that makes me love you more and more. I'm proud to say "that's my son!"

Through the years, I've tried to take care of my family and give them some of the better things in life. I tried and succeeded in being able to give my children a good education. Although I was only a working man, many was the time I worked two jobs for the extra money so that the family could have a little bit more. I had often thought of going into some kind of business, but I didn't have the expertise in any particular field, or the finances to afford the luxury of risk. However, I'm proud to say that you have shown me through the years, the aggressiveness that I lacked emerged in you.

I have tried to be financially sound and leave behind an adequate amount of finances to carry your mother through the rest of her days. Being no one can predict the future, I ask that should it ever be necessary, see that your mother remains comfortable financially and otherwise.

Leigh, you have always made me proud with your accomplishments and different endeavors. You have never undertaken a task that was under-achieved. Through the years you have been in my confidence and as close as a daughter. I love you and the girls deeply.

My concentration is not too great at this point as I'm sure I can say much more. Keith could not have picked a finer mate. You are a good wife and excellent mother. I feel a father and daughter relation to you.

I hope Danielle and Michelle follow in the footsteps of the family and their traditions. I love you all.

Dad

There are many similarities between an ethical will and a personal mission statement. The author of this document developed his personal mission statement over more than 5 years. It serves the same purpose as an ethical will although the style is less narrative than the previous examples.

My mission is to serve God by creating a balance between family, friends, profession, and community.

1. I will be guided by the teachings of Judaism.
2. I will act on situations and opportunities, rather than be acted upon.
3. I will not make assumptions of what people need. I will ask
4. I will be a fair and honest evaluator of situations.
5. I will be positive. I will look for the good.
6. I will be courageous and persistent to experience and accept differences.
7. I will be sincere, yet decisive
8. I will remember that one person **can** make a difference.
9. I will share. In sharing, one learns, experiences, and reaps the highest level of satisfaction.
10. I will keep a sense of humor.
11. I will not fear mistakes, for mistakes are the springboard of future success.

With family and friends, I will seek to understand first before being understood. I will be empathic, which is sympathy with a solution. Sometimes that solution is just to listen. I will be supportive and inspiring, attempting to assist those within my circle of influence to become interdependent people. My wife and children are my highest priority with regard to creating this positive interpersonal relationship.

Professionally, I will help people devise and implement financial and personal plans to afford these people financial and emotional independence. I will be honest and always put a client's best interest ahead of my financial reward. This is with the understanding that I must make an income to be able to service clients. I will only ask a client to do something that I do or hope to do once sufficient capital is acquired. The best investment one can make is in oneself and other people. I will run a profitable business with equal emphasis on providing a positive work environment as well as profitability.

To my community, I will allocate a minimum of 10% of my money and time. One are of focus will be in building bridges between Jews and non-Jews. My other area of focus will be with youth in 7th through 12th grade, helping to develop and implement programs which will help them to acquire the leadership skills necessary to become interdependent and effective adults.

My personal dreams today are:

1. Have a meaningful and special relationship with my wife.

2. Raise responsible children.

3. Help people who demonstrate a caring for others, reach their goals.

4. Become a philanthropist.

5. Teach other financial planners this business.

6. Enjoy the people and the process.

Additional notes:

1. What is hateful to you do not do on to others.

2. Act as if all your actions will be part of a story published in the Wall Street Journal.

Being a parent:

The goal of being a parent is to guide the child from ignorance to wisdom, from moral neutrality to virtue, from dependency to interdependence, from infancy to maturity. My goal as a parent is to prepare the child to function as an independent adult in an interdependent society.

My obligation is to:

1. Teach ethical and moral behavior

2. To have you wed

3. To teach you a craft (a means to make your own income)

4. Teach you to swim

5. Practical citizenship so that you may function as an upright and productive member of society

Selected References and Resources

Ethical Wills: Putting your values on paper, by Barry K. Baines, MD, Perseus Publishing, 2002

Women's Lives, Women's Legacies: Passing Your Beliefs and Blessings to Future Generations: Creating your spiritual-ethical will, by Rachael Freed, Fairview Press, 2003.

From Age-ing to Sage-ing, by Zalman Schacter-Shalomi and Ronald Miller, Warner Books, 1997

Tuesday s With Morrie by Mitch Albom, Doubleday, 1997

Kitchen Table Wisdom, by Rachel Naomi Remen, M.D. Riverhead Books, 1996.

So That Your Values Live On, Ethical Wills and How to Prepare Them by Jack Riemer and Nathaniel Stampfer, Jewish Lights Publishing, 1991.

Man's Search for Meaning, by Viktor Frankl, Simon and Schuster, 1959,1962,1984

Ethical Will Web Site

www.ethicalwill.com More than 30 modern ethical wills are posted on this site.

Josaba Ltd.

A Minneapolis-based company that will print your ethical will on archival quality paper and place it in an archival quality keepsake folder for storing and preserving your ethical will. For more information, call 612-374-9526.

About the Author

Barry K. Baines, MD is an alumnus of Brooklyn College, with a degree in Psychology, and a graduate of Georgetown University School of Medicine. He is a family physician and currently serves as the Chief Medical Officer of UCare Minnesota and as the Associate Medical Director of Hospice of the Twin Cities, a home-based hospice program in the Twin Cities of Minneapolis and St. Paul, Minnesota.

Barry's interest in Ethical Wills began when his father developed a terminal illness in 1990. However, it was his hospice care experiences that provided the impetus for developing the Ethical Will Resource Kit. This kit is designed to help people write and preserve their legacy of values.

NOTES

NOTES